Visions of ICELAND

Scenes and Surprises from Land and Sea

Photos by Páll Stefánsson
with an Introduction by Steinunn Sigurdardóttir

Iceland Review

Visions of Iceland
Introduction: Steinunn Sigurdardóttir
Photographs and picture captions: Páll Stefánsson
English translation: Bernard Scudder
Design: Erlingur Páll Ingvarsson
Lithography: Prentmyndastofan hf., Reykjavík
Printed in Portugal
Published by Iceland Review © Reykjavík, Iceland 1996
Reprinted in 1999
Front cover: Hraunfossar in Borgarfjördur
Map of Iceland © Landmælingar Íslands

The photos were taken with Leica M6, Leica R6.2 and
Linhof 612 PC11 cameras on Fuji Velvia film

ISBN 9979-51-106-0

INTRODUCTION

The Icelandic landscape is a challenging subject to capture, whether in words or images, because it is a realm where instability rules supreme, both on the surface and below it. In this respect the whole country is like the Jökulsárlón glacial lagoon, where icebergs change shape and shift from one minute to the next. A tourist lucky enough to capture a cloudless photo of Mt. Hekla could not have come five minutes later, because Icelandic clouds are incredibly quick off the mark. More to the point, Hekla, like many other mountains in Iceland, is a fairly unstable character: you can never tell whether it won't be erupting on the next photo you take of it.

Peaceful villages snuggling in the shelter of mountains, like Hveragerdi, can suddenly start shaking and trembling without the slightest warning, and such earthquakes can spawn new hot springs, even in the middle of what was previously a sitting-room floor.

There are some photographers who have a knack of capturing the mountain a minute before the volcanic cloud erupts from its crater, the cloud before it changes direction, the iceberg before it splits, the village an instant before the earthquake invites it to a pas-de-deux. Imminent action of this kind is the subtext of Páll Stefánsson's photographs of Iceland. And the tension between it and absolute tranquillity.

As it happens, one of the characteristics of Iceland is that the peace reigning there, which is so great, and the silence which is so dense, are something greater than mere tranquillity and silence. Within the Icelandic landscape, threat and mystery are never far off. This is part of the explanation for the enchantment that the land exerts, even though it is virtually devoid of anything apart from landscape in solid and liquid form. Nor is it any small area, either, that the landscape occupies and unfolds to welcome its visitors. This huge island, a whole one-fifth larger than Ireland, is the most sparsely populated country in Europe with only 2.65 inhabitants per square kilometre. By comparison, the most densely populated country, the Netherlands, has 140 times as many people per square kilometre. Even the only real city, Reykjavík, with its 106,000 inhabitants, is "a drop in the ocean" alongside the average metropolis – and has large areas, too, whose character is natural rather than urban.

Iceland could never become densely populated, because glaciers cover twelve percent of its surface, and the harsh winter realm of the highlands will always be inhospitable to settlement. But alongside the shore, on the lowland plains of the south and southwest, and in valleys and on moors, Icelanders have made their homes for the eleven hundred years since they sailed their boats across the ocean from Norway, carrying their cargo of seasick cattle. One of the island's peculiarities is how scant evidence there is of the settlement that is recorded in such detail in stories and sagas. Most buildings in Iceland are brand new, "as if everyone there had just flown in on the last plane," as author Pétur Gunnarsson put it.

The Icelanders have certainly shown an exceptional inaptitude for building monuments to themselves from permanent and tangible materials, and a unique feature of the country is the fact that its ancient relics are almost entirely made from words and stories. This is one reason why the traveller in Iceland will always find something to occupy his or her mind: the landscape is a book. With their grand heritage of stories through which they can trace their descent back to the kings of Norway, Icelanders have always made a habit of taking the unprovable literally, so that the landscapes where saga heroes lived and rode and fought are shrines of a sort, even though no material sign of them remains today. And for visitors who have no knowledge of the exact story the landscape has to tell, there is no lack of inspiration for mental fiction or fantasy.

Every place has a name in Iceland. Some sites still have the same names they were given by saga heroes when the settlement began, and the unpopulated parts are in fact populated, too, by place names. A strange-looking rock is given a name, the tiniest brook is called something. This must surely reflect some kind of respect for the land, love for it, and desire to take care of even the minutest of landmarks. The wealth of place names tells of a struggle for survival so tough that it almost finished the nation off for good, and of a yearning for a more tender place to call home. In a country where the forces of nature take such a high toll in human lives, it is not surprising to find a cliff called Líkkista ("Coffin") or a lake called Líkárvatn ("Corpse River Lake"), nor that the longing to satisfy a craving stomach should create a place called Unadsdalur ("Valley of Pleasure") or Smjörvatn ("Butter Lake"). The combined effect of the sagas and the place names associated with them is to make the vast and empty Iceland into a country with the densest population of stories anywhere in the world.

One of the great luxuries of moving around in this vast domain of stories is its physical space, the absence of people. Even in the peak tourist season at a popular tourist spot such as Skaftafell National Park, you only need to turn the corner to be sure that no one is there, and doubly sure if you turn the next corner after that.

Islands are sometimes said to magnify claustrophobia. Admittedly Iceland is surrounded by the sea on all sides, but nonetheless it leaves an impression of being a continent rather than an island. People in Iceland are more likely to be seized with agoraphobia than claustrophobia, because the clear air and raw, richly coloured landscapes create views that seem to stretch almost endlessly in all directions.

For all the room there is to move within it, the land needs to be treated with much more caution than it has been shown until now. Icelandic nature is extremely fragile, the vegetation is sensitive and highly susceptible to disruption. Everything that takes root in Iceland does so at an exceptionally slow and hesitant pace, because the growing season is so short and the climate unfavourable: cold, windy and not sufficiently humid.

In recent years there has been a noticeable national awakening aimed at re-clothing the land, which was described in ancient chronicles as being "covered with woodland from mountain to shore" at the time of the settlement. Afforestation work and staying in chalets in the cosy shelter of woodland are increasingly popular ways of coming into contact with nature and, so to speak, establishing a constructive peace settlement after centuries of battling with the elements. Yet even if all able-bodied Icelanders were to spend their time planting trees for all they were worth, it would take a long time before Iceland came anything close to being half-clad. In fact, its nudity is one of the qualities that make the land at once enchanting and unwelcoming.

The character of the land is elusive and ever-changing. All that we see and the camera captures is not what the land is, but what it has just become, its endless interplay with various states of light. The flickering brightness that lights up the land strives either to strip it even barer or to clothe it in a veil. It contributes to the interaction between the lucid and the nebulous that instils travellers with such an obsessive love that some, at least, could head around the Ring Road a thousand times over without ever tiring of it. The clouds, the colours of the land and the light offer the eye new marvels to wonder at each time they combine. And anyone who risks going out of town in winter may end up witnessing a firework display far away from the city lights: a starlit sky with a flood of northern lights rippling across it from one end to the other.

With a combination of insight, talent, patience and luck, a good photographer can re-produce some of these wonders with incredible accuracy. To the uninitiated, they are revealed like visions. And those who are familiar with the land can even scent it there in the cold, pure North Atlantic air that gives the lungs a good cleaning out, some-times with a dash of sulphur. That is the special gift of a photographer such as Páll Stefánsson – the paradox of capturing the hidden qualities of the land, not to enslave them but to liberate them.

Steinunn Sigurdardóttir

Reykjavík

ENDLESS VIEW

Few capitals in the world can boast panoramic views to match
Reykjavik's beautiful semicircle of mountains and vast,
enchanting seascape. Glittering on the horizon
to the northwest is the mystical crown of Snæfellsjökull
glacier, atop an extinct volcano. It may look close enough
to reach out and touch, but the glacier is actually 100km away
across the blue Faxaflói bay.

HOT SPOT

Naturally hot water keeps outdoor swimming pools warm all year round. Swimming is a national pastime, or obsession: Reykjavik's pools check in 1,500,000 bathers a year, equivalent to everyone in the city taking about one dip a month. Laugardalur pool is the largest in the city.

BAY WATCH

Skerjafjördur bay on Reykjavík's southern side is probably
the best place in the country for boating.
Hundreds of youngsters are initiated there into what, in this
country of fishermen, may become their livelihood.
In the background is the popular Öskjuhlíd recreation area,
crowned by the space-age structure of the Pearl.

THE CITY'S HEART

*The lake, Tjörnin, by whose shores the old village grew into
a city, is Reykjavik's gentle heart. In the lakeside City Hall,
opened in 1992, municipal business nestles
and takes wing — taking its cue from the lake's fellow citizens, the
birds that nest there and bring joy and colour
to the lives of city-dwelling nature lovers.*

THE LIVING PAST

*Up until almost the middle of this century, people lived at the
old farm of Árbær on the outskirts of Reykjavík. In 1957 it
was converted into an open-air folk museum to house
all manner of articles from times gone by.
Old houses from various periods have been moved there in
their entirety, and special events there every summer bring
the spirit of the past back to life.*

NATIONAL DAY

Reykjavík walks tall with a carnival air on National Day, June 17.

HIVE OF LEARNING

In many schools, final-year students go out in style — in fancy dress.

THE PEARL

*On Öskjuhlíd hill stands the Pearl, a glass dome cupped
over the geothermal water distribution tanks that have
provided Reykjavík with central heating since 1930.
Although Reykjavík means "Smoky Bay," the city
is totally smoke-free; its name refers to geothermal steam.
The top floor of the Pearl is a revolving restaurant with a
panoramic view worthy of such an eye-catching landmark.*

REFLECTIVE REYKJAVÍK

Lakeside buildings genuinely reflect the city's character: the pure white walls of the National Gallery, the quietly dignified Fríkirkja — the Free Lutheran Church — and the corrugated-iron-clad school where Reykjavík children were taught the 3 R's well into this century. On the hill above them towers the spire of Hallgrímskirkja, the biggest church in Iceland.

MIDNIGHT SEA

Reykjavík is by far the largest port in Iceland, with two separate harbours. The older one is home to a thriving fishing industry, while the new harbour handles most of the cargo for the whole of Iceland. And the port is active around the clock. The richly coloured sun means that this oil tanker is being piloted to dock at midnight.

THE WATERFRONT

Even at midnight the entrance to the old harbour is an ideal place to catch a breath of fresh air and maybe even a fish, or just to ponder how modern buildings have been transforming the shoreline in recent years.
Reykjavík is a rapidly growing city and is now home to 106,000 people, about 40% of the population of Iceland.

FREEDOM

*Exploring the uninhabited wilds on horseback is a popular
leisure activity among Icelanders and visitors alike.
This party in Dómadalur valley in the south central highlands
is returning from an invigorating three-week trek
with only each other, their horses and the raw elements
for companionship.*

LONE RANGER

Threading his way along Jökulgil in the south central highlands, this lone horseman looks like a pawn on nature's infinitely intricate chessboard. For centuries, the Iceland Horse was the only means of transport between farms or districts. Even today the sure-footed Iceland Horse with its characteristic five different gaits is the best form of travelling through nature, nature's way.

UP AND AWAY

The most popular spot for highland travellers has always been
Landmannalaugar, where clusters of tents in summer give it
the look of a cosy village. But this is a place to start out from,
not to settle in. Its gloriously coloured landscapes stretching as
far as the eye can see make Landmannalaugar a whole new
world to relax in, reflect and regenerate.

THE SOFTER SIDE

Countless hiking trails in the highlands stretch out from
Landmannalaugar, past stunning landmarks such as the
colourful Mt. Brennisteinsalda. Here, at 750 metres above
sea level, the snow never manages to melt completely,
but nestles down into a landscape where rivers and streams
have sculpted the soft rhyolite mountains.

SHEEP ROUNDUP

*From the end of May to autumn, sheep are set free to range
and graze in the mountains and valleys, far from the world
of man. Before winter descends they are rounded up and
herded back to the farms, which can be an arduous task.
These farmers from Landsveit, south Iceland,
go both on foot and on horseback to reclaim their flocks from
nature's tempting pastures.*

RAINBOW'S END

*Laugafell, on the northern side of Hofsjökull glacier,
is a tiny oasis of green grass and hot springs in a desert of
black sand. For centuries this was a resting place on the main
track where people travelled on foot between north and south
Iceland, and today the Touring Club of Iceland maintains a
mountain hut at Laugafell.
There is no cold water — even the toilet uses hot water!*

FREE TO ROAM

*The reindeer is one of Iceland's few wild mammals. It is not a
native species, but was imported from Norway late in the
eighteenth century, and has roamed free in nature ever since.
Mainly concentrated in the eastern highlands, reindeer add
a noble presence to the land they have made their own.*

SLUMBERING SECRET

Beneath this tranquil, moss-covered landscape below
Mt. Sveinstindur lies an awesome secret. In 1783, the hundred
or so craters of Lakagígar erupted to produce
the largest lava flow ever witnessed in historical times
anywhere in the world, which spread over almost 600km²
of land and caused a haze as far away as Asia.

WET THRILLS

The thrills and spills of river rafting in the powerful river Hvítá.

R O A D   T O   N O W H E R E

Mountains and rough terrain are no obstacle to cyclists.

RED FALLS

East of Mt. Hekla, the peculiarly fanning Raudifoss ("Red Waterfall") is a true treasure of nature. Beautifully coloured stones glitter like jewels on the river bed, originating from the rhyolite massif of Raudufossafjöll, whose highest peak reaches 1,230m.

DETTIFOSS

Dettifoss (44m) on the river Jökulsá á Fjöllum is more than just the most powerful waterfall in Europe, with an average flow of almost 200m³ of water per second. It is also the meeting point of contrasts: thunderous noise and unspeakable motion in an otherwise calm and solid landscape — watching its raging force soothes the mind.

NATURE'S SCULPTURE

Jökulsárgljúfur, downriver from Dettifoss, is the most dramatic canyon system in Iceland, 25km in length and 100m deep in places. The surrounding 150km² site, declared a national park in 1973, is like a gallery of nature's unique art, such as the magnificently sculpted Tröllid ("The Troll") in the "echoing cliffs" of Hljódaklettar.

A S K J A

Askja lake lies in a caldera where the land has sunk after an eruption in the Dyngjufjöll mountains in 1875, which also gave birth to the crater (foreground) called Víti – "Hell." At 217m, Askja lake is the deepest lake in Iceland, and a place where the elements obey rules of their own – the unpredictable weather can also produce the finest summer days anywhere in the country.

HEAVENLY HELL

*Still lukewarm more than a hundred years after the eruption
that created the crater of Víti ("Hell"),
the water there can be devilishly tempting. Of all Iceland's
natural hot springs, this must surely be the strangest
— sheltered by a 60m crater wall, its water cloudy and
sulphurous, and worth clambering down to for the sheer joy
of relaxing after the effort.*

N E W L Y   M A D E   L A N D

Steaming hot lava at Krafla, a fissure near Lake Mývatn that last
erupted in 1984.

STILL GOING STRONG

Hekla gives one of its periodic eruptions, in 1991.

COLD HEAT

The Kverkfjöll mountains on the northern edge of Vatnajökull glacier are a living natural paradox. At almost 2,000m above sea level, hot springs bubble at the rim of the glacier. Warm streams melt the glacier to form long caves of ice inside it, which eventually collapse to be replaced by others elsewhere. There is a mountain hut at Kverkfjöll and also an airstrip for private planes, the highest and most remote in the country.

BOILING POINT

Unearthly views unfold from Mt. Námafjall near Lake Mývatn in the north. At Hverarönd, one of the largest solfatara areas in Iceland, geothermal activity has transformed the land into bubbling hot springs and simmering mud pots. The earth's crust is precariously thin under foot — and there's hot action going on beneath it!

ALONG
THE COAST

JUMPING GIANT

The seas around Iceland are teeming with whales — fifteen species have been documented. The day that this 30-ton, 17-metre humpback did some unexpected acrobatics in Skjálfandi bay in the north, its smaller cousins turned up to watch too: minke whales, dolphins and killer whales.

BUSY OUTPOST

Langanes, Iceland's northeasternmost extreme, bustles with colourful seabird life. Kittiwake, fulmar and eider have colonies there, and on the skerry Karl ("Old Man"), gannet, guillemot and kittiwake live and lay their eggs side by side, in peace and harmony.

ARCTIC KING

The King Eider visits its realms in Iceland every year,
although it nests elsewhere.

W H O ' S C O M I N G ?

The colourful, appealingly pompous puffin stands guard everywhere.

STOPOVER

The calm lagoons of Lón in the southeast offer passing swans shelter from both men and the cold ocean waves.
Swans congregate here to compare notes before flying off to their winter homes in warmer southerly climes, and make their first call here in spring when they return.

RICH PROVIDER

Bolungarvík is one of numerous towns and villages snuggled
up for shelter against sheer mountains in the West Fjords.
Since the first days of the settlement eleven hundred years
ago, people here have harvested the sea, which is often
more of a challenge than on this calm summer day.
Today, Bolungarvík's 1,100 inhabitants play a major role
in Iceland's vital fish export industry.

INVISIBLE BORDER

At the northernmost point of Melrakkaslétta, you can stand
where Hraunhafnartangi juts out into the Atlantic Ocean
and look across to the other side of Arctic Circle,
over the border of the inhabitable world.

GROWING PORT

Grindavík on the Reykjanes peninsula in the southwest is an
old trading post; it has been growing rapidly and now ranks
with the leading fishing ports in Iceland. Its natural harbour
was once difficult to negotiate from the open sea,
but has since been upgraded.

HOME SWEET HOME

A trawler returning to its home port of Dalvík in Eyjafjördur, north Iceland.

PLOUGHING THE WAVES

Dredging for scallop in Breidafjördur bay, west Iceland.

HUNTER AT HOME

Thórdur Halldórsson from Dagverdará on the Snæfellsnes peninsula, a legend in his lifetime — famed for his exploits as a fisherman and fox-hunter.

L A U G H I N G   M A T T E R

Kolbrún, aged four, all aglow at play in the evening sun.

RHAPSODY IN BLUE

The Blue Lagoon on the Reykjanes peninsula is one of the
most popular tourist attractions in Iceland, drawing some
130,000 visitors every year. Formed by pure and hot runoff
water from the nearby geothermal power station,
it is rich in minerals that are healthy for the skin.
By the bathhouse the temperature is a comfortable 35-40°C.

WATER WALL

*Water takes on countless guises as it interacts with the land.
One of the many impressive waterfalls in south Iceland,
Seljalandsfoss literally stands out from the landscape beside
the Ring Road — you can walk behind it, under the ledge
where it plummets down from the mountainside.*

ICEBERGS AHOY

When Vatnajökull, the largest glacier in Europe, began to retreat from the shore in the warmer climate after 1950, it left behind a lagoon around 100 metres deep which is filled with ice-cold meltwater, where calving icebergs head out to sea. Cruising in this chilly, dreamlike world, dwarfed by the icebergs, man marvels at the grandeur and magnitude of nature.

RISE AND SHINE

During summer, it is bright all day in Iceland, and all night too.
The sun barely sets before it has risen again. All living things
rejoice in the nightless world of the north.

TOP CONTRASTS

South of Vatnajökull lies Skaftafell, one of Iceland's three national parks. For centuries it was isolated by roaring glacial rivers on either side. The opening of the Ring Road in 1974 brought travellers flocking to admire its magical contrasts of rugged rock, moraine and woodland. Above it, clad in the white mantle of the glacier, towers Hvannadalshnjúkur, the highest peak in Iceland at 2,119 metres above sea level.

COLOURFUL
REUNION

*Every autumn, farmers round up their horses from mountain
pastures to bring them back to farms for the winter.
In Skagafjördur in the north, it's a colourful event when
farmers reclaim their own trusty horses from the corral.
Iceland Horses come in many distinctive hues
and are traditionally named after them.*

NORTHERN LIGHTS

*To brighten up the darker, cooler winter nights, dazzling
northern lights dance wildly across the firmament before a
captive audience on the earth below. Their ceaseless movement
and riot of colour light up the sky here above
Breiddalsvík on the east coast.*

WARMING SMILE

Akureyri, the largest town in north Iceland with a population of 15,000, is the national centre for winter sports and also one of the most important industrial and fishing towns in the country. Preschool children on a walk around the town centre certainly received a smiling winter welcome.

ICY MOVE

Vatnajökull glacier is the largest ice cap in Europe, measuring 8,400km² in area. In 1994 and 1995, two glacial tongues surged from it at speeds of up to 100m a day. Onlookers are dwarfed by the ice piled up along the 30km stretch where the Tungnaárjökull glacial tongue has surged to create walls up to 80m high in places.

GLACIAL CANYONS

*The plane looks like a mere speck beside the gigantic natural
architecture produced by a glacial surge.
When the Síðujökull glacial tongue surged, crevasses
stretched 30km back from its rim into the Vatnajökull ice cap.
Volcanic and geothermal forces are at work beneath the ice
cap and Grímsvötn, at its centre, is one of Iceland's
most active central volcanoes.*

SNOW MOTION

It can be fun outdoors in winter, if you dress up to keep out the cold.

PEACEFUL LIFE

A fisherman in Hjalteyri on Eyjafjördur fjord strolls home after a fine day's catch.

CAMOUFLAGE

The island of Hrísey in Eyjafjördur fjord is home to 300 people, almost all of whom live by fishing. This 11.5km² island is a thriving sanctuary for birds, in particular the ptarmigan. And like the ptarmigan, Hrísey wears white for the winter.

SUSPENSE

Svartifoss is surely the most distinctive of the many waterfalls in Skaftafell National Park, with basalt columns that frame it like organ pipes. And it is no less magnificent in winter, hung with its decoration of ice.

TWILIGHT ZONE

Winter travellers need to proceed with caution. They need to be ready for all types of weather, because storms can engulf the land in an instant. And when they do, man is left entirely to his own resources in remote places such as Hvalvík on the northeastern Melrakkaslétta coast.

L A N D M A R K

By Hvalsnesfjall mountain at Lón on the southeastern
corner of Iceland, the peaks stand out proudly.
Their claim to fame is that they were the first sight glimpsed,
from the sea, by the first Vikings when they sailed over from
Norway eleven centuries ago.

S N O W B I T E

There's nothing to beat a bite of waiter-service hay when the grass is blanketed with snow.

CAUGHT BY FROST

*Frozen fishing gear in Húsavík harbour, awaiting the fishermen who
in their own way have been hardened by the elements.*

WHITE-OUT

*Wild storms are fortunately fairly rare in the settled parts of
Iceland, but everyone can expect at least one onslaught a year,
such as this blizzard at Skagaströnd in the northwest.
Storms can be fierce enough to smash electricity pylons,
completely cutting off certain places from civilization.
But the Icelanders have learned to live with the elements
and will soon restore everything to normal.*

CURTAIN OF SNOW

The spire of Hallgrímskirkja church in Reykjavík is an ideal place for panoramic views from the capital — except in a snowstorm on a cold winter's day. Across the bay, the usually distinctive Mt. Skardsheidi is lit by a vague glint of sunshine.

KEEPING WATCH

Whatever the weather, the Reverend Fridrik Fridriksson
— founder of the YMCA and a promoter of youth work
and sports — keeps a caring watch around his statue.
But when the cold northern wind roars through the city
of Reykjavik, most people choose to stay indoors.

C L A I R
D E   L U N E

The moon peeps up above the sheer face of Lómagnúpur, one of the highest cliffs in Iceland at almost 700 metres. This landmark, the boundary between south and east Iceland, stands out from afar, towering above the southeastern sands of Skeidarársandur.

I C E L A N D

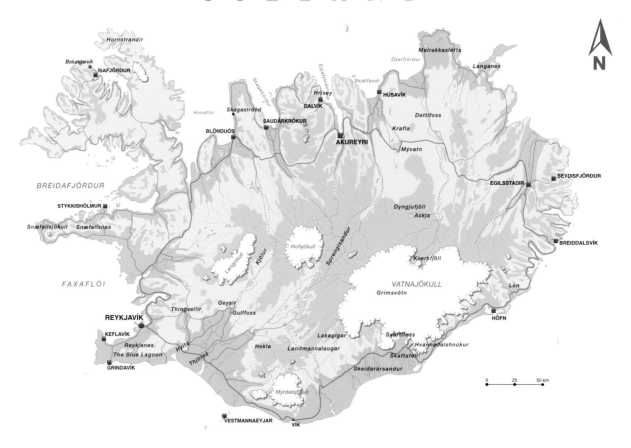

On this map are shown all of the main places mentioned in this book.